W9-AZG-417

2/20 8w

True Survival

THE ROBERTSON FAMILY

ATTACKED BY ORCAS

Virginia Loh-Hagan

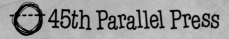
45th Parallel Press

Published in the United States of America by Cherry Lake Publishing
Ann Arbor, Michigan
www.cherrylakepublishing.com

Reading Adviser: Marla Conn MS, Ed., Literacy specialist, Read-Ability, Inc.
Book Cover Design: Felicia Macheske

Photo Credits: ©Christian Musat/Shutterstock.com, cover; ©DiegoMariottini /Shutterstock.com, 5; ©De Visu/
Shutterstock.com, 7; ©Jack R Perry Photography/Shutterstock.com, 8; ©nd3000/Shutterstock.com, 11;
©BlueOrange Studio/Shutterstock.com, 12; ©Tory Kallman/Shutterstock.com, 14; ©Dudarev Mikhail/
Shutterstock.com, 17; ©piola666/iStock.com, 19; ©anas sodki/Shutterstock.com, 20; ©JueWorn/Shutterstock.com,
23; ©Rich Carey/Shutterstock.com, 24; ©Andrey_rage/Shutterstock.com, 27; ©Thinglass/Shutterstock.com, 29

Graphic Elements Throughout: ©Gordan/Shutterstock.com; ©adike/Shutterstock.com; ©Yure/Shutterstock.com

45th Parallel Press is an imprint of Cherry Lake Publishing.

Library of Congress Cataloging-in-Publication Data has been filed and is available at catalog.loc.gov

Cherry Lake Publishing would like to acknowledge the work of The Partnership for 21st Century Skills.
Please visit *www.p21.org* for more information.

Printed in the United States of America
Corporate Graphics

table of contents

chapter one

Off to See the World!

Who were the Robertsons? Why did they sail around the world?

The Robertson family was special. They were lost at sea. They lived through it. This happened in 1971.

There were six members of the Robertson family. Dougal was the father. Lyn was the mother. Douglas was the oldest son. He was 18 years old at the time. Anne was 17 years old. Neil and Sandy were twins. They were boys. They were 9 years old.

Dougal was a **merchant navy** officer. He was a hired sailor. He **retired** from sailing. Retired means he stopped working. But he still ran a farm. He did this for 15 years.

Dougal had sailed in East Asia.

spotlight biography

Jose Salvador Alvarenga is a fisherman. He sailed from Mexico to El Salvador. He did this in 2012. A storm hit his fishing boat. The storm lasted 5 days. Alvarenga was lost in the Pacific Ocean. He was lost for 13 to 16 months. He was trapped in his fishing boat. He lost his fish. He lost his tools. He lost his radio. He had traveled with a friend. But the friend died at sea. Alvarenga was far away from people and cities. He survived by eating turtles, birds, sharks, and fish. He drank rainwater. He saw the Marshall Islands. He left his boat. He swam to shore. This happened in 2014. Two people found him. They took him to the hospital. Alvarenga was the first person to survive in a small boat lost at sea for over a year. Some people didn't believe his story.

The Robertsons had a **dairy** farm. Dairy is milk and cheese. The farm was in England. It was far away from other cities and people. It didn't have running water. It didn't have power. It wasn't doing well. The Robertsons were losing money.

Douglas said, "Dad's life was terrifically hard. He was very **frustrated**. He saw his brothers and sisters sending their children off to university and private school, the sorts of things he was no longer able to provide." Frustrated means upset.

Neil asked why they couldn't sail around the world like Robin Knox-Johnston. Knox-Johnston was an English sailor. He sailed around the world.

Robin Knox-Johnston was the first to sail around the world nonstop and by himself.

Dougal loved the idea. He wanted to show his family the world. He wanted to sail with his family. He wanted them to learn at the "university of life." He was ready to escape the farming life.

Lyn wasn't so sure. She was worried. She knew the trip would be dangerous. She hoped Dougal would change his mind. But Dougal sold the farm. He bought a boat. He used all their money.

The boat was named *Lucette*. It was 43 feet (13 meters) long. It was a wooden **schooner**. Schooners are a type of sailboat.

◄ Schooners have two or more masts. Masts are poles that hold sails.

chapter two

Attacked by Killer Whales

What was sailing like for the Robertson family? Why did they have to abandon ship?

The Robertson family set sail on January 27, 1971. They left from Cornwall. Douglas said, "Father's planning for this journey was zero. We didn't even have a practice sail around the bay before setting off around the world." Dougal was the only family member with sailing experience. He knew about big boats. He didn't really know much about smaller boats.

At first, the trip was fun. Dougal was at the wheel. He'd stomp on the floor. He'd shout, "Yee-haw!"

But the fun didn't last. The family sailed into a storm. Douglas said, "We suddenly got an **inkling** this wasn't going to be a walk in the park." Inkling means idea.

Before sailing on big trips, people should practice for a while.

The Robertson family quickly learned how to sail. They learned how to use all the ropes. They learned how to move the sails. They had no choice.

They sailed across the Atlantic Ocean. They did this for a year and a half. They stopped at different places. They stopped in the Caribbean. Anne didn't want to travel anymore. She left the family in the Bahamas.

The Robertsons sailed to the Panama Canal. They picked up a student named Robin Williams. Williams didn't have a lot of experience sailing. But he wanted to travel.

The Caribbean islands are off the coast of Florida.

explained by
science

Some people use saltwater to heal cuts. Some people use saltwater to fix skin problems. Some people gargle with saltwater to heal sore throats. Doctors use saline. Saline is special saltwater. It's sterile. Sterile means clean. Saltwater from the ocean isn't clean. It has all kinds of things in it. The world is getting warmer. This means there's more deadly germs in oceans. This makes seawater dangerous. It's not good for cuts. So, people should use saline not seawater. Salt forces liquids in cells to move out of the body. It forces bad germs out of the body. It dries out cells. This is how saltwater cleans cuts. But don't drink saltwater. This can make people thirstier.

They were close to the Galapagos Islands. They were in the Pacific Ocean. A **pod** of **orcas** hit their boat. Pod is a group. Orcas are killer whales.

The whole boat shook. Part of the boat cracked. Douglas said it sounded like a tree trunk being snapped in two. He heard the orcas splashing around him. He thought he was going to be "eaten alive."

The boat sank. Dougal yelled, "**Abandon** ship!" Abandon means to leave. The Robertsons and Williams got into the rubber life raft. They didn't have time to grab anything.

◄ Wild orcas have no interest in hurting humans.

chapter three

Stuck in a Boat

**What were the crew's chances for survival?
What was *Ednamair*? What was their plan?**

The orcas finally left. But the **crew** was stuck. Crew refers to the people in the boat. The Robertsons and Williams were in the middle of the ocean. Lyn was still in her nightgown.

There was no hope for rescue. They weren't on a shipping path. Ships weren't coming by. They wouldn't be seen. Nobody knew they were missing. Nobody would be looking for them.

They only had enough water for 10 days. They had enough food for 6 days. They had a bag of onions. They had a box of biscuits. They had 10 oranges. They had six lemons. They had a small bag of candy. Survival was slim.

They watched their boat sink. It took minutes.

would you?

- **Would you sail around the world?** Sailing around the world is fun. It's great to see different places. But it's a lot of work.

- **Would you drink turtle blood?** Turtles move slowly. So, they're easy to catch. People drink turtle blood. They eat turtle meat. They eat turtle organs. They eat turtle eggs. But turtles need to be protected. Some species are endangered.

- **Would you go to the Galapagos Islands?** The Galapagos Islands have a lot of wildlife. They have wildlife not seen anywhere else. They have many plants. They have many animals. Over 170,000 people visit each year. People can only visit certain parts. There are only a few flights on and off the islands.

The rubber life raft had a leak. Water came up to their chests. They got sores. They couldn't sleep. Their heads hit the water. They were afraid of drowning. The rubber life raft broke after 17 days.

They moved to a **dinghy**. A dinghy is a small boat. It's often used as a lifeboat. The dinghy was named *Ednamair*. It was only 10 feet (3 m) long. It wasn't that strong. There was too much weight for the small boat. Water came in. They were worried about sinking. They took turns sitting in the dry spots.

They sucked on rubber. This made spit. It helped them be less thirsty.

The Robertsons were far away from land. They wouldn't make it. So, Dougal came up with a plan. He said, "If we sailed to the middle of the Pacific where there was regular rain and more chance of rescue, we could collect rainwater and at least stay alive." That's what they did. Dougal made a mast out of an oar. They used the winds. They wanted to catch the waves to the United States.

The Robertsons and Williams fought a lot. But they also learned to work together. They shared food. They shared jobs. They took turns watching for dangers. They took turns sleeping.

◄ When sharks would circle, Dougal would punch them to scare them away.

chapter four

Saved by Turtle Blood

What did they eat? How did they use turtles to survive?

The Robertson family learned to live off the ocean. They ate fish. They ate sharks. Sometimes, fish would be in sharks' stomachs. They ate that too. Douglas said, "It would taste as if it had been cooked in a grill."

But they mainly ate turtles. In fact, turtles saved their lives. Douglas said, "You wouldn't believe how hard it is to kill a turtle with your bare hands. The first ones I caught I had to let go. They fight hard and slash you with razor-sharp claws." They learned. They caught 13 turtles. They tied them up. They bled their necks.

They made a spear from an oar.

They needed water to survive. They stayed hydrated by drinking turtle blood.

They ate turtle meat. They ate turtle eggs. They drank turtle blood. They dried its meat. They stored it.

They collected turtle fat. They let the fat heat in the sun. They made turtle oil. They rubbed it on their skins. This helped their sores. It also kept water out. The family drank turtle oil. This kept them warm.

Water at the bottom of the dinghy was poisonous. It was a mix of rain, blood, and turtle guts. It was bad to drink. Lyn was a nurse. She made a tube. She poured the dinghy water in their rear ends. This way, they could absorb the water. But poison didn't go through their bodies.

survival tips

TRAPPED AT SEA WITH A GROUP!

- Choose a leader. This person should know the most about survival. The leader should assign jobs to everyone.

- Collect all items. See what can be used to survive.

- Use clothes or plastic bags. Make a roof or cover. Keep out of the sun.

- Count the food supply. Sort food into small portions. Make it last. Share food evenly with everyone.

- Signal for help. Use mirrors or lights. Make flags by attaching bright clothes to sticks.

- Share blankets. Huddle with others. Do this to keep warm. Nights can get cold.

- Move around to keep blood moving. Shake your legs. Shake your arms.

- Take turns sleeping. Save energy. Rest when you can. Stay quiet.

chapter five

Rescued at Last!

How long were they lost at sea? How were they rescued? What happened after their rescue?

The Robertsons and Williams survived for 38 days. They were finally rescued on July 23, 1972.

The *Toka Maru II* was a Japanese fishing boat. It was sailing to the Panama Canal. The fishermen saw the *Ednamair*. They didn't think there'd be any survivors. Then, they saw a **flare**. Flares are light. The fishermen went to save the family. The family jumped up and down. Their tongues had swollen up. They couldn't speak. But they were very happy.

Douglas said, "My dad had been sunk once before . . . by the Japanese in 1942. And here they were in 1972 picking him out of the water and saving his life."

The *Ednamair* was 300 miles (483 kilometers) from land.

Rest in Peace

Karp Lykov was Russian. He belonged to the Old Believers. This is a group of really religious people. They were punished by the country's new government. The government killed Lykov's brother in 1936. So, Lykov ran away. He escaped with his family. The Lykovs moved far away from the city. They lived deep in the Siberian forests. They lived on a mountain. They lived in a log cabin. They lived away from other people for over 40 years. They didn't see another human being. They had a hard time surviving. They used trees for clothes and shoes. They ate bark. Four of the five children died. One child, Agafia Lykov, lived. She was the only remaining family member. She was taken to a hospital to fix her leg. But she returned to her forest home. Scientists discovered them in 1978.

The Robertsons and Williams were taken to Panama. Douglas celebrated. He ate three big breakfasts. He ate steak, eggs, and fries.

The Robertsons moved to an aunt's farm. Then, Dougal and Lyn got a divorce. Dougal bought another boat. He lived in the Mediterranean. He got sick. He died in 1992. He had cancer. Lyn went back to farming. She nursed Dougal before he died. She also got sick. She died. Douglas joined the navy. Then he became an **accountant**. Accountants keep track of money. Douglas has no regrets. He's proud to be a survivor. He said, "Life is **precious**." Precious means special.

Their story was in many newspapers. They were famous.

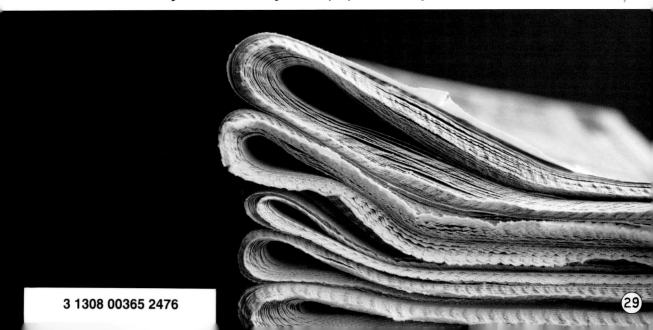

Did You Know?

- Dougal Robertson was born in Edinburgh, Scotland. He was born in 1924. He was the youngest of eight children. He went to Leith Nautical College. Nautical means of the sea. Dougal's first wife and son died. Lyn was his second wife. Dougal met Lyn in Hong Kong.

- Dougal Robertson wrote a book about his family. The book is called *Survive the Savage Sea*. It covers the days after the shipwreck. It's based on the ship's logs. Logs are notes kept while sailing.

- In 1992, there was a movie about the Robertsons' survival. Douglas Robertson said the movie is loosely based on facts. He said, "They sailed from Australia, not England!"

- Douglas Robertson wrote a book about his family. The book is called *The Last Voyage of the Lucette*. He wrote it in 2005. But not many people know about it. Douglas couldn't promote his book. His son almost died in a motorbike accident. So, Douglas had to take care of his son.

- The Robertsons were scared of orcas. But wild orcas rarely attack humans. Captive orcas have killed humans.

- Wild orcas attacked the *Lucette*. They probably thought the boat was another whale.

- Douglas said you have to drink turtle blood quickly. Otherwise it can turn thick. Douglas said it has an "aftertaste that makes you want to retch." Retch means to throw up.

- The crew tied their water tanks together. They hung them off the side of the boat. A turtle cut the rope with its claws. This happened on the 23rd day.

- The Robertsons gave *Ednamair* to a museum. Over 400,000 people have seen it.

Consider This!

Take a Position: The Robertsons ate sea turtles in order to survive. Is it okay to eat endangered animals in order to live? Endangered means these animals are at risk for disappearing. Argue your point with reasons and evidence.

Say What? Read the 45th Parallel Press book about Steven Callahan. Compare Callahan to the Robertsons. Explain how they're alike. Explain how they're different.

Think About It! Read more about orcas. Compare captive and wild orcas. Do you think they're a threat to humans? Why or why not?

Learn More

- Klepeis, Alicia Z. *Orcas on the Hunt*. Minneapolis: Lerner, 2018.
- Long, David, and Kerry Hyndman (illust.). *Survivors: Extraordinary Tales from the Wild and Beyond.* London: Faber and Faber Children's, 2016.
- Spilsbury, Louise A. *Surviving the Sea.* New York: Gareth Stevens Publishing, 2016.

Glossary

abandon (uh-BAN-duhn) to leave

accountant (uh-KOUN-tuhnt) a person whose job is to track money

crew (KROO) workers on a ship; a group of people

dairy (DAIR-ee) having to do with milk and cheese from cows

dinghy (DING-ee) a small boat often used as a lifeboat

flare (FLAIR) a rescue device that makes a bright light

frustrated (FRUHS-tray-tid) upset or annoyed

inkling (INGK-ling) idea

merchant navy (MUR-chuhnt NAY-vee) hired sailor

orcas (OR-kuhz) killer whales

pod (PAHD) a group

precious (PRESH-uhs) special, of great value

retired (rih-TYRD) having left one's job after a certain amount of time

schooner (SKOO-nur) a type of sailboat with two or more masts

Index

About the Author

Dr. Virginia Loh-Hagan is an author, university professor, and former classroom teacher. She wrote part of this book in the library of Owens Intermediate School in Bakersfield, California. So, this book is dedicated to the wonderful students at Owens. She lives in San Diego with her very tall husband and very naughty dogs. To learn more about her, visit www.virginialoh.com.